THE STATES AND THEIR SYMBOLS

Colorado
Facts and Symbols

by Emily McAuliffe

Content Consultant:
Eugene Hainer
Sr. Consultant, School Library Development
Colorado State Library

Hilltop Books

An Imprint of Franklin Watts
A Division of Grolier Publishing
New York London Hong Kong Sydney
Danbury, Connecticut

Hilltop Books
http://publishing.grolier.com

Library of Congress Cataloging-in-Publication Data
McAuliffe, Emily.
    Colorado facts and symbols/by Emily McAuliffe.
    p.cm.--(The states and their symbols)
    Includes bibliographical references and index.
    Summary: Presents information about the state of Colorado, its nickname,
motto, and emblems.
    ISBN 1-56065-764-2
    1. Emblems, State--Colorado--Juvenile literature. [1. Emblems, State--
Colorado. 2. Colorado.] I. Title. II. Series: McAuliffe, Emily. States and their
symbols.
CR203.C6M38
978.8--DC21   978.8   97-40418
                                     MCA   CIP
                                     1-03   AC
                                     1351951

Editorial credits:
Editor, Cara Van Voorst; additional editing, Kim Covert; cover design, Clay
  Schotzko/Icon Productions; illustrations, James Franklin; photo research,
  Michelle L. Norstad

Photo credits:
Dembinsky Photo Assoc. Inc., cover; Gary Meszaros, 12
Robert McCaw, 18
Charles W. Melton, 14
One Mile Up Inc., 8, 10 (inset)
Unicorn Stock Photos/Andre Jenny, 6, 10; Ron Holt, 16; Gurmankin/Morina, 22 (top),
  Deneve Feigh Bunde, 22 (middle); Dick Young, 22 (bottom)

Table of Contents

Fast Facts about Colorado

Capital: Denver is the capital of Colorado.

Largest City: Denver is the largest city in Colorado. More than 400,000 people live in Denver.

Size: Colorado covers 104,100 square miles (270,660 square kilometers).

Location: Colorado is in the western United States. It is bordered by Wyoming, Nebraska, Kansas, Oklahoma, New Mexico, Arizona, and Utah.

Population: 3,822,676 people live in Colorado (U.S. Census Bureau, 1996 estimate).

Statehood: Colorado became the 38th state on August 1, 1876.

Natural Resources: People in Colorado mine coal, gold, oil, uranium, and natural gas.

Manufactured Goods: Coloradans make foods, computers, aircraft, and machinery.

Crops: Colorado farmers grow wheat, hay, corn, beans, sugar beets, and peaches.

State Name and Nickname

Colorado is a Spanish word that means red. Spanish explorers saw a river of reddish water in Colorado. An explorer travels an area to discover what it is like. The river flowed through deep valleys of red stone. The explorers named it the Colorado River. Later, people chose Colorado as the state's name.

People call Colorado the Centennial State. Centennial means the 100th year. The United States became a country in 1776. Colorado became a state 100 years later.

Another nickname for Colorado is the Highest State. Some of Colorado's mountains are more than 14,000 feet (4,267 meters) high. Mount Elbert is the highest point in Colorado. It is 14,433 feet (4,399 meters) high.

People also call Colorado the Switzerland of America. Switzerland is a country in Europe. Switzerland is famous for its mountains.

Colorado has many high mountains. These mountains are in the Rocky Mountain National Park.

State Seal and Motto

The state seal is a symbol. A symbol is an object that reminds people of something larger. For example, the U.S. flag reminds people of the United States.

The state seal is a small picture pressed into wax. Government officials stamp the seal on important papers. The seal makes government papers official.

Colorado adopted its state seal in 1877. The seal shows a picture of an eye. The eye is a symbol of God watching over people. Mountains and mining tools appear on the seal. Miners found gold in Colorado's mountains in 1858.

Colorado's state motto is Nilsine Numine. This means Nothing Without Providence. A motto is a word or saying. Providence means help from God. Colorado's motto says that nothing can happen without God's help.

Colorado adopted its state seal in 1877.

State Capitol and Flag

Denver is the capital of Colorado. A capital is the city where government is based.

The capitol is in Denver. Government officials work in this building. Some officials make laws for the state. Others make sure the laws are carried out.

Workers completed Colorado's capitol in 1908. They spent 22 years building it. The capitol has a gold dome. A dome is a roof shaped like half of a globe. A thin layer of real gold covers the dome.

Colorado adopted its state flag in 1911. The flag has two blue stripes and one white stripe. The blue stripes stand for sky. The white stripe stands for mountain snow. A red letter C appears in the middle of the flag. It stands for Colorado. There is a gold circle in the middle of the C. It stands for the gold discovered in Colorado's mountains.

Colorado's capitol is in Denver.

State Bird

The lark bunting is Colorado's state bird. It became the state bird in 1931. Lark buntings are about six inches (15 centimeters) long. They have gray, black, and white feathers.

Lark buntings help farmers. The larks eat grasshoppers. Grasshoppers harm crops. The larks also eat grain. They eat grain that farmers throw away.

Lark buntings fly in large groups. They fly south for the winter. They return to Colorado in April.

Male larks fly a special way to court female larks. Males fly high in the sky so females notice them. Then they drift slowly down to Earth. They sing as they fly up and down.

Sometimes people say that a person is happy as a lark. People say this because larks seem very happy.

Lark buntings have grey, black, and white feathers.

State Tree

The Colorado blue spruce became Colorado's state tree in 1939. Colorado students chose the tree. A blue spruce can grow 115 feet (35 meters) high.

The blue spruce is green and silver-blue. It has pine cones and short, sharp needles. A thick wax coats the blue spruce's needles. This wax gives it a silver-blue color.

The Colorado blue spruce grows wild in the Rocky Mountains. The Rocky Mountains is a mountain range in Colorado. An explorer discovered the Colorado blue spruce on Pikes Peak in 1862. Pikes Peak is a famous mountain in the Rocky Mountains. A peak is the pointed top of a mountain.

Many people plant the Colorado blue spruce in their yards. Companies make paper and boxes from the tree's wood. People often choose blue spruce trees for Christmas trees.

A blue spruce can grow 115 feet (35 meters) high.

State Flower

Colorado's state flower is the Rocky Mountain columbine. This columbine is white and lavender. Lavender is a light purple color.

The Rocky Mountain columbine became the state flower in 1899. It grows about 10 inches (25 centimeters) high.

Each columbine flower has five petals. Petals are the colored outer parts of flowers. The petals are mostly white with spots of lavender. Other types of columbines have blue, red, or yellow petals.

The petals of the columbine form hollow tubes. The tubes hold nectar. Nectar is a sweet liquid found in flowers. Hummingbirds and bumblebees collect nectar from the tubes.

Colorado government officials passed a law about picking columbines. People may pick no more than 25 in one day.

Each Rocky Mountain columbine flower has five petals.

State Animal

The state animal of Colorado is the Rocky Mountain bighorn sheep. It became the state animal in 1961. Bighorn sheep weigh up to 300 pounds (135 kilograms). They can live up to 20 years.

Male bighorn sheep have huge horns. Their horns curve back and down close to their heads. Some horns curl in a complete circle. The horns grow as long as 50 inches (127 centimeters).

Rocky Mountain bighorn sheep live in the Rocky Mountains. They live near rocky cliffs. Their sharp hooves help them climb the cliffs. Bighorn sheep have good balance. They are also skilled jumpers. They can jump from one cliff to another.

Rocky Mountain bighorn sheep have many enemies. Coyotes, cougars, grizzly bears, and wolves hunt the sheep. The bighorn sheep often escape by running up steep cliffs. Their enemies are not able to follow them.

Rocky Mountain bighorn sheep live in the Rocky Mountains.

More State Symbols

State Fish: The greenback cutthroat trout is the state fish. But there are not many of these fish left. The greenback cutthroat is in danger of dying out.

State Folk Dance: The square dance is the state folk dance. Square dancers follow directions called out by a leader.

State Fossil: The stegosaurus is the state fossil. The stegosaurus was a plant-eating dinosaur.

State Grass: Blue Grama is the state grass. Blue Grama grass grows wild throughout Colorado.

State Insect: The Colorado hairstreak butterfly is the state insect. This butterfly has purple wings with black and orange markings.

State Song: "Where the Columbines Grow" is the state song. A.J. Fynn wrote the song. Colorado government officials chose the state song in 1915.

The Colorado hairstreak butterfly is Colorado's state insect.

Places to Visit

Mesa Verde National Park

Mesa Verde National Park has ancient cliff dwellings. A dwelling is a place where people live. The Anasazi people built their homes in the sides of cliffs. They left the cliff dwellings about 800 years ago. Park visitors tour the dwellings. The largest one has more than 200 rooms.

Glenwood Hot Springs Pool

Glenwood Hot Springs Pool is a huge outdoor swimming pool. The pool is heated by hot springs. A hot spring is a natural supply of hot water. The water is heated inside the earth. People can swim in the warm pool all year. Steam rises from the pool during the winter.

Rocky Mountain National Park

Rocky Mountain National Park is near the city of Estes Park. Many of the park's mountains are more than 10,000 feet (3,048 meters) high. Longs Peak is the highest mountain in the park. It is 14,256 feet (4,345 meters) high. Deer, elk, and Rocky Mountain bighorn sheep live in the park.

Words to Know

centennial (sen-TEN-ee-uhl)—the 100th year
dwelling (DWEL-ing)—a place where people live
explorer (ek-SPLOR-ur)—a person who travels to discover what a place is like
fossil (FOSS-uhl)—the remains of an animal or plant that lived long ago
insect (IN-sekt)—a small animal with six legs
motto (MOT-oh)—a word or saying
nectar (NEK-tur)—a sweet liquid found in flowers
petals (PET-uhls)—the colored outer parts of flowers
symbol (SIM-buhl)—an object that reminds people of something larger

Read More

Bledsoe, Sara. *Colorado*. Minneapolis: Lerner Publications, 1993.

Bock, Judy and Rachel Kranz. *Scholastic Encyclopedia of the United States*. New York: Scholastic, 1997.

Fradin, Dennis B. *Colorado*. From Sea to Shining Sea. Chicago: Children's Press, 1993.

Petersen, David. *Rocky Mountain National Park*. Chicago: Children's Press, 1993.

Useful Addresses

Colorado Historical Society
1300 Broadway
Denver, CO 80203

Colorado Secretary of State
1560 Broadway, Suite 200
Denver, CO 80203

Internet Sites

A Brief Guide to State Facts
http://phoenix.ans.se/freeweb/holly/state.html#colorado
50 States and Capitals
http://www.scvol.com/States/main.htm
State of Colorado - Kids Page
http://www.state.co.us/kids/index.html

Index